Photosynthesis

Titles in The KidHaven Science Library include:

Atoms

The Big Bang

Cells

Chemical Reaction

Cloning

Computers

Diabetes

Electricity

The Extinction of the Dinosaurs

Genetics

Germs

Gravity

The Immune System

The Internet

Lasers

Light

The Mars Rovers

Microscopes

Molds and Fungi

Molecules

Motion

Plate Tectonics

Space Travel

Thunderstorms

Tide Pools

Tornadoes

Volcanoes

Weather

The KidHaven Science Library

Photosynthesis

by Bonnie Juettner

KIDHAVEN PRESS

An imprint of Thomson Gale, a part of The Thomson Corporation

THOMSON

™

GALE

Detroit • New York • San Francisco • San Diego • New Haven, Conn. • Waterville, Maine • London • Munich

For more information, contact
KidHaven Press
27500 Drake Rd.
Farmington Hills, MI 48331-3535
Or you can visit our Internet site at http://www.gale.com

LIBRARY OF CONGRESS CATALOGING-IN-PUBLICATION DATA

Juettner, Bonnie.
    Photosynthesis / by Bonnie Juettner.
        p. cm. — (The KidHaven science library)
    Includes bibliographical references and index.
    ISBN 0-7377-2350-5 (hardcover : alk. paper)
    1. Photosynthesis—Juvenile literature. I. Title. II. Series.
    QK882.J84 2005
    572'.46—dc22

                                                            2004021972

Printed in the United States of America

Contents

Chapter 1

Leaf Factories

A plant may have just a few leaves, or thousands. No matter how many leaves a plant has, each leaf has the job of making food for the plant. This job is called **photosynthesis**. Photosynthesis means "putting together with light." To make food for a plant, leaves put raw materials together. The raw materials are carbon dioxide, a gas, and water, a liquid. To change the raw materials into food, plants also need energy—the energy of sunlight.

Chemical Changes

Photosynthesis is a **chemical process**. A chemical process is one in which substances change into other substances. This is like what happens when a cook bakes a cake. A cook might use flour, eggs, sugar, and other ingredients as raw materials. Then he or she places the ingredients, well mixed, into an oven. The oven provides energy in the form of heat and causes a chemical change to take place. When the cook removes the pan from the oven, it no longer contains the separate ingredients flour, eggs, or sugar. It contains a cake.

Plants also go through chemical changes. Their ingredients are carbon dioxide and water. Energy for their chemical transformation comes from sunlight. All of these ingredients—carbon dioxide, water, and sunlight—must enter a plant through its cells.

Water is one of the three ingredients all plants need to perform photosynthesis.

How Photosynthesis Works

Chlorophyll in the plant absorbs light energy from the Sun.

1

The leaves give off oxygen and water vapors.

6

The leaves absorb carbon dioxide from the air.

2

Light, carbon dioxide, water, and nutrients are used to make sugars. The plant uses these sugars for food.

5

The roots absorb water (3) and minerals and nutrients (4) from the ground.

3

4

Cells

All living things are made of **cells**. Some very tiny living things are made of just one cell, but plants and animals are made of many cells. Cells are so tiny that most can be seen only through a microscope.

Water enters a plant through the cells in its roots. Then the water travels up through cells in the plant's stem. These cells form pipes that provide the water with a path all the way to the leaves, where photosynthesis will take place. Carbon dioxide and sunlight, however, can enter the plant directly through the cells in its leaves.

One leaf of one plant may easily contain tens of thousands of cells. Not all the cells in a leaf are alike, however. The cells on the top surface of the leaf are clear and thin. Sunlight can pass directly through these cells to reach the cells in the middle of the leaf, where photosynthesis takes place. Carbon dioxide, however, must pass through holes in the cells.

Guard Cells and Stomata

The holes in a plant's cells are called **stomata**. On either side of the stomata lie **guard cells**. The guard cells regulate the stomata, making sure that they open and close as needed. In most plants, this means making sure the stomata are open during the day, when sunlight is available for photosynthesis, and closed at night. One green plant needs billions of open stomata to let carbon dioxide in, because only a small percentage (0.03 percent) of Earth's air is composed of carbon dioxide.

Guard cells have another important function. While letting carbon dioxide in, they work to make sure that not too much water gets out. This keeps plants from drying out. When the stomata are open, the water in the plant cells can evaporate, or warm up so much that it becomes a vapor and enters the air. Normally this process is called evaporation. In plants, it is called **transpiration**.

The cells on the surface of a leaf must allow some transpiration to occur, because this process uses up heat energy and cools the plant on warm days. (Human skin cells do the same thing. They cool the skin by allowing water to exit and evaporate into the air. In humans, this process is called perspiration, or sweating.) Plants normally sweat, or transpire, large amounts of water. For example, one corn plant may lose 440 pounds (200kg) of water in a few months through transpiration. An acre of corn will lose 1,320 pounds (60kg).

A plant cannot survive, though, if it transpires too much water. Plant cells are 90 percent water. (Plants need even more water than humans, who are more than 60 percent water.) If a plant does not contain enough water, it will wilt, because water pressure helps plants to keep their shape. Just as important, water is one of the raw materials used in

Plant Cell

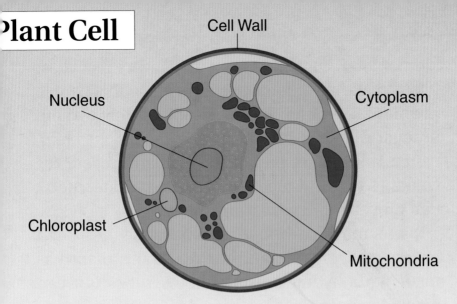

Cell Wall

Nucleus

Cytoplasm

Chloroplast

Mitochondria

Plant cells contain a nucleus, the genetic control center. Mitochondria convert sugars into energy and float in a liquid jelly called cytoplasm. Chloroplasts contain chlorophyll, which is used in making the plant's food supply. A plant cell's firm walls are made of cellulose.

photosynthesis. Plants cannot make food out of carbon dioxide alone.

Plant Food

Once the leaves of the plant have all the ingredients they need—carbon dioxide, water, and sunlight—they can begin photosynthesis. They use the energy of sunlight to bring about a chemical transformation in the water and carbon dioxide. Water contains hydrogen and oxygen, while carbon dioxide contains carbon and oxygen. Once photosynthesis has taken place, the carbon dioxide gas and liquid water are no longer there. The hydrogen, carbon, and some of the oxygen have been transformed into a kind of food, sugar. However, the sugars that most plants make are different from the sugar that people put into cakes or on cereal. Most plants make a kind of sugar called fructose. Apples, bananas, zucchini, carrots, pumpkins, and other fruits and vegetables contain fructose. Fructose is a **carbohydrate**, a food that provides energy to living things.

Plants make carbohydrates because they need energy to live, grow, and thrive. After a plant has made carbohydrates using photosynthesis, it can break down the sugar to provide itself with energy for growing new leaves. It can also use that energy to grow stems, roots, seeds, pollen, and flowers. All

The fruit in this market all contain fructose, a sugar that many plants make as a source of energy.

together, Earth's plants produce, or grow, a vast amount of new living matter—about 176 million tons (160 million metric tons) every year.

At the same time that photosynthesis produces sugar, it also releases oxygen. Water and carbon dioxide both contain oxygen, but to make sugar, plants need only some of that oxygen. Plants release their extra oxygen into Earth's atmosphere.

Importance of Photosynthesis

Earth did not always have oxygen in its atmosphere. Scientists believe that 2.5 billion years ago, blue-green algae on the surface of Earth's seas began to photosynthesize. Just like plants today, the algae used water, carbon dioxide, and sunlight. And just like plants today, they released their leftover oxygen into Earth's atmosphere. Slowly the composition of the atmosphere began to change. Today it is almost 21 percent oxygen. (Earth's atmosphere is mostly nitrogen and also contains argon, carbon dioxide, and tiny amounts of several other gases.) Humans and other animals depend on plants to provide the oxygen in our atmosphere.

People and animals also depend on plants for food. In addition to making sugars during photosynthesis, plants make proteins and starches. Even carnivorous predators who eat only meat could not survive if their prey, or their prey's prey, did not have plant foods to eat.

Humans depend on the oxygen that plants like the trees in this rain forest produce during photosynthesis.

Because photosynthesis is so important, scientists dream of finding a way to duplicate it. So far, however, they have not been able to do so. No animal can make its own food, as plants do. Only plants can convert water, carbon dioxide, and sunlight into food and oxygen for the living creatures of Earth.

Chapter 2

Seasonal Changes

Plants do not do photosynthesis in the same way all year round. During the summer, much more sunlight is available for photosynthesis than during the winter. Plants must adapt to changing weather conditions. They need just enough light. If they get too little they cannot grow and thrive. But if they get too much they will wilt, because too much water will transpire out of the leaf cells into the air.

Spring and Summer

Spring and summer are a time of growth for plants. During the spring, plants that drop their leaves in the winter begin to grow new leaves. The leaves will be solar collectors for the plant during the summer, when light is abundant. Every plant has different leaves. However, most leaves have certain characteristics in common. They are thin and flat, so that light can pass through the surface cells to reach the cells in the middle of the leaf. Leaves are shaped more like sheets of paper than like soccer balls, because light could not penetrate a ball-shaped leaf very easily.

Although almost all leaves are thin and flat, their shapes vary. Some are oval, while others are shaped more like feathers, arrows, hands, or needles. Most plants have broad leaves, like the leaves on maple trees and on most flower bushes. But some plants, such as grasses and grains, have long, narrow leaves. Evergreen plants, such as pine and spruce trees, have needle-shaped leaves.

Plants grow their leaves in locations where they can collect as much light as

Pictured here are oval shrub leaves (below), pine needles (left), and a maple leaf (above).

possible. The leaves on a tree branch will grow in places where they will cast as little shadow as possible on other leaves. The leaves on a plant's stem typically will form a spiral around the stem. Sunflower leaves, for example, do this. Some plants, though, have leaves that grow in pairs on opposite sides of the stem. One pair might grow on the north and south side of the stem, with another pair on the east and west side of the stem. However, if the light available to the plant comes only from one side, the leaves may grow primarily on that side. This sometimes happens when a houseplant is placed in a window.

Fall Colors

In the fall, the leaves of some plants change color and fall to the ground. Trees that drop their leaves in

Fall in New York's Central Park is a beautiful sight as the leaves on the trees change color.

Unable to perform photosynthesis in fall and winter, deciduous trees survive on food they have stored throughout the summer.

the fall, such as maple and oak, are called deciduous. Leaves change to red, yellow, orange, or brown in the fall because of how they do photosynthesis.

Plant cells involved in photosynthesis contain tiny organs called organelles. The organelle where photosynthesis occurs is called a **chloroplast**. Chloroplasts are so small that a section of the leaf the size of three grains of salt can contain hundreds of thousands of chloroplasts. Each chloroplast contains a pigment called **chlorophyll**. Chlorophyll looks green and gives leaves their green color. Chlorophyll is the part of the plant cell that stores the energy of sunlight. But chloroplasts also contain some yellow-orange pigments, called carotenoids. Scientists believe that carotenoids help to disperse extra light, which might otherwise damage the chlorophyll.

When nights begin to be cool and days get shorter, it is time for photosynthesis to end for a while—at least in deciduous plants. When this happens, the chlorophyll in deciduous plants starts to break down. As the green chlorophyll in the plant's leaf cells breaks down and disappears, the green color of the leaf fades away. The carotenoids, however, do not break down. Their yellow-orange color remains. And in some leaves, new pigments called anthocyanins form as chlorophyll decays. Anthocyanins can make leaves look red or purple. As the leaves turn to yellow, orange, red, or purple, they begin to fall from the tree.

Winter Cold

It makes sense for deciduous trees to shed their leaves in the winter when there is less sunlight and colder temperatures. Tree leaves can survive freezing that occurs outside their cells, but not freezing that occurs inside their cells. The leaves of deciduous trees are so thin that they can easily freeze all the way through. To avoid this, deciduous trees drop their leaves. Some plants lose not only their leaves but even their stems, relying only on underground root systems to get them through the winter.

Because deciduous trees go through the winter without leaves, they must also go through the winter without conducting photosynthesis. They must make and store enough food in the summer to last them through the fall and winter. Food for trees, as for other plants, is the sugar, or fructose, that they make during photosynthesis. Plants store fructose temporarily in their chloroplasts. Later they move the fructose to their seeds, roots, or stems and keep it there until they need it.

Other plants, however, do manage to conduct photosynthesis during the winter. They do less photosynthesis than they do in the summer, because there is less sunlight and often less water available for them to work with. In evergreens photoynthesis takes place year-round. Their leaves stay green through the winter, which is how evergreens got their name. An evergreen's leaves resist freezing because they are shaped like needles. Some other plants, such as holly, have leaves with waxy surfaces that protect them from the cold. These leaves can do winter photosynthesis as well, although they sometimes curl up a little in response to the cold.

Winter poses a challenge to most plants, but it is a challenge that comes to an end when spring returns and temperatures rise. When this happens, plants can do photosynthesis again, building up

The leaves of the holly bush have a waxy coating that provides protection from the cold.

food supplies that may have grown low during the winter. Some plants, though, live in climates where water or sunlight are scarce year-round. These plants must adapt to their climate to survive.

Chapter 3

When Water Is Scarce

Nobody knows exactly how many different kinds of plants there are, but scientists have identified at least 260,000. Plants live almost everywhere on Earth. Many plants live in places where they have more to cope with than just the changing of the seasons. Some plants live in places where there is very little water, or where the temperature gets so high that they are in danger of losing much of their water through transpiration. When their environment makes it difficult to survive, plants must adapt.

Desert Plants

Deserts are an especially difficult habitat for plants. In deserts, water is scarce because little rain falls—less than 10 inches (254mm) per year. What rain does fall evaporates quickly in a desert's high daytime temperatures. In deserts, temperatures can rise above 100 degrees Fahrenheit (38 degrees Celsius) during at least part of the year. At these temperatures, rain sometimes evaporates into the air before it hits the ground.

Plants living in less dry environments tend to shut down photosynthesis during hot, dry weather. They can survive occasional days or weeks without photosynthesizing much because they live in climates that are not dry all the time. Plants living in deserts, however, do not have the option of stopping photosynthesis whenever the weather is very hot and dry. The weather is hot and dry most of the time, and they must still make food for themselves.

Some plants, such as corn and sugarcane, can store carbon dioxide in spaces within their leaves.

Farmers harvest sugarcane, a plant that stores carbon dioxide in its leaves.

This way, they can collect carbon dioxide when their stomata open and continue to do photosynthesis using stored carbon dioxide even after the stomata close. As a result, these plants are able to keep their stomata closed for at least some of the hot daytime hours.

Some succulents such as these cacti have no leaves and perform photosynthesis in their stems.

Other plants, called **succulents**, have developed their ability to store carbon dioxide even more. Succulents can open their stomata and collect carbon dioxide mostly at night. Then they can keep their stomata closed during most of the day, conducting photosynthesis using the stored carbon dioxide. Cacti and aloe are succulents. When their stomata are closed, the surface of these plants is almost waterproof. They lose very little water through transpiration. Succulents reduce their loss of water even more by limiting the surface area of their leaves. Cacti have no leaves at all (photosynthesis takes place in their stems). Other succulents have just a few leaves or have leaves that drop during the driest season of the year.

Even when a plant loses very little water, it must still get water somehow. Succulents can absorb a lot of water in a very short time during the occasional rainfall because they have wide, shallow root systems. For example, the roots of a saguaro cactus (a plant that grows in the Sonora Desert of Arizona and Mexico) are nearly as wide as the saguaro is tall. Once it has collected all the water that it can from a rain, the cactus stores it for future use in photosynthesis. To protect its water supply from thirsty animals, a cactus has sharp spines.

Succulents can absorb water only when the soil is thoroughly soaked. Other desert plants, however, have other strategies. Some, such as the mesquite tree, have very deep roots extending as far as 80 feet

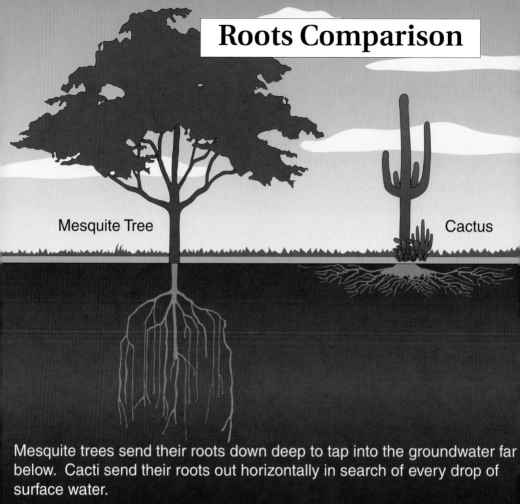

Mesquite Tree

Cactus

Mesquite trees send their roots down deep to tap into the groundwater far below. Cacti send their roots out horizontally in search of every drop of surface water.

(24m) below the surface of the ground. These plants can become dormant, or sleep, through very dry periods. When there is enough rain to wet soil that is deep underground, plants like these come out of dormancy and begin to grow. By the time the soil is that wet, they can expect to have enough water to conduct photosynthesis for several weeks before entering dormancy again.

Deserts also support another kind of plant, called a drought avoider. Desert wildflowers fall into this category. Wildflowers avoid dry periods altogether. They do not bother to survive drought. Instead, they drop seeds and then die. The seeds can remain dormant until the next rainfall, in some cases even if the next rainfall does not occur for ten years. When enough rain falls, a new plant can grow from the seeds that were left.

Prairie Plants

Plants living in prairies, or grasslands, face some of the same challenges to photosynthesis that desert plants encounter. They must withstand dry weather and high temperatures. Even though prairies exist in some of the world's drier climates, they do get about three times as much rain as deserts do. But prairie plants often lose water to transpiration when they are blown by the wind. Prairie plants get little enough water that they must adapt in some of the same ways that desert plants do.

Like some desert plants, grasses have thin, narrow leaves. Leaves that have this shape lose less water to transpiration than broad leaves do. Grasses and wildflowers, like some desert plants, also have deep root systems. Some prairie plants have fuzzy leaves that keep the plant cooler by reflecting more sunlight. Others have leaves that roll up on dry days to avoid transpiring too much water.

Prairie plants also face a danger that is less common in the desert: fire. Prairies tend to be covered

Prairie grasses protect themselves from grazing animals like bison by storing most of their food in stems underground.

with dry grass, which catches fire easily from lightning strikes during thunderstorms. During a fire, prairie grasses burn completely. A fire can clear an area of most of its grass in just a few hours. It may seem as though being burned to the ground would completely destroy a plant. However, prairie grasses keep only one-third of their growth above ground.

A fire that burns grasses to the ground still leaves two-thirds of the plant intact, protected under a layer of soil. This two-thirds of the plant includes not just its root system but also underground stems, called **rhizomes**.

When prairie grasses conduct photosynthesis, they store some of the food that they make in their rhizomes, where it is safe from fire and other dangers (such as animals that graze on grass). These grasses can sprout up quickly after a fire. So can some prairie trees and shrubs, such as aspen and some oaks. Oaks also have another adaptation to their environment. They have thick bark that resists burning and protects the interior of the oak's trunk. Although the oak's leaves may burn, they can re-sprout quickly, just as the prairie grasses can. Some prairie plants have adapted so well to the reality of

Fire burns across a section of California woodland. The thick bark of these oaks offers protection from fire.

occasional fires that they grow back thicker than ever after a fire.

Plants adapt to extreme environments for their own benefit, so that they can survive, thrive, and reproduce. But many desert animals rely on the water that is stored in succulent plants. Prairie grasses, with their dense root system, hold topsoil in place, preventing it from being washed away by rain and wind. Farmers need this topsoil to grow their crops. By adapting to extreme environments, plants make it possible for people and animals to survive and thrive in those environments too.

Chapter 4

When Sunlight Is Scarce

Some plants must adapt to climates in which there is little sunlight. Plants growing near Earth's North Pole and South Pole must live with a scarcity of water and sunlight. Plants also live in and under water, where sunlight is scarce.

Polar Temperatures

Polar plants include plants that live in the Arctic and plants that live in Antarctica. Because these areas get less sunlight than the rest of Earth, temperatures in the Arctic range from –60 degrees Fahrenheit (about –51 degrees Celsius) in the winter to about 50 degrees Fahrenheit (10 degrees Celsius) in the summer. It is so cold so much of the time that, under the few inches of soil that defrosts in the summer, the ground is permanently frozen. The permanently frozen part of the ground is called permafrost. The land areas where permafrost exists are called **tundra**. Antarctica is even colder than the Arctic.

Temperatures there rarely rise above freezing and can get as low as –94 degrees Fahrenheit (–70 degrees Celsius). Antarctica is almost entirely covered with ice and snow.

Both polar regions get less rain and snow than deserts do. (The Arctic is wetter than Antarctica in the summer, because at that time of year water that was locked in snow melts into bogs. But in the winter this water freezes again and is not available to plants.) Polar regions are also very windy. Antarctic winds sometimes reach 120 miles (193km) per hour. Wind this strong can hasten water loss in plants.

A polar bear makes its way across the frozen tundra of its Arctic home.

Seeking Out Sunlight

But perhaps the biggest challenge for polar plants is the lack of sunlight. These regions alternate between months of nearly twenty-four-hour daylight and months of nearly twenty-four-hour darkness. Although plants cannot conduct photosynthesis without sunlight, at least seventeen hundred species of plants manage to survive in polar regions.

How do plants adapt to such a forbidding environment? To begin with, they downsize. Trees do not grow near the poles because their roots cannot penetrate the permafrost. The plants that do grow are small. In the Arctic tundra, mosses, lichens, wildflowers, and small bushes can grow. These plants can survive with a shallow root system. In Antarctica, plant life is limited to mosses and lichens that can cling to rocks, and very small plants that can float in the ocean.

Staying small and close to the ground offers polar plants some protection from winds. This is important, because polar plants must conserve water for use in photosynthesis. Wind can increase the transpiration of water from the leaves of plants. These plants also have small leaves, which further reduces the amount of water that they transpire. (The bigger a leaf is, the more water it loses through transpiration.)

A polar plant's biggest challenge, though, is to collect enough energy from sunlight. In milder climates plants may spread out their branches to give their leaves the chance to collect sunlight from a larger area. But in the Arctic and in Antarctica, plants frequently must grow huddled together in clumps to help protect themselves from the cold. And polar plants must confine themselves to growing during the summer, when there is light available for photosynthesis. This gives them a growing season of only about sixty days. During those sixty days, sunlight is available nearly constantly, but the Sun stays low in the sky so its light is less intense.

To make the most of the few hours of low-intensity sunlight that they get, many Arctic plants have adapted by growing leaves that are dark red rather than green. Dark red leaves absorb more light than green leaves do. (Dark colors absorb more light; lighter colors reflect more.) Some grow flowers in the shape of a bowl, to absorb more heat and retain it longer. Many have hairy stems, to help them stay warm longer, just as animals in cold climates have fur to help keep them warm. The most common adaptation of polar plants, however, is that they grow very slowly. Not all polar plants flower every year. Some take years to prepare for flowering.

Taiga

Just south of the region of tundra near the North Pole, and in a few parts of the Andes mountain system of South America, lies an area known as **taiga**.

Growing in clumps helps moss in Antarctica to survive the freezing cold.

In taiga regions, plants face many of the same challenges that polar plants do. They get more sunlight, though they still must cope with long hours of darkness in the winter. Taiga regions also contain some

Because sunlight in taiga regions is very limited, evergreen trees growing there must conserve their energy.

permafrost, but not enough to stop trees from growing. The trees that grow in this area are mostly evergreens.

Evergreen trees, like polar plants, must conserve their energy because the amount of sunlight available for photosynthesis is so limited. They do not drop their leaves in winter, the way deciduous trees do. That way, they need not expend energy growing new leaves in the spring. Instead they can begin photosynthesis right away. Evergreen leaves are shaped like needles to reduce water loss through transpiration, because in the winter, water is scarce. (To people and animals, water does not seem scarce in the winter. That's because people and animals can eat snow. Trees cannot.) Evergreen needles are dark green, which absorbs more sunlight, just as the dark red leaves of polar plants do.

Underwater Plants

Polar plants are not the only vegetation to survive in an environment without much sunlight. Underwater plants too must survive with limited exposure to light. Sunlight's intensity is reduced so much when it travels through water that underwater plants are classified as shade plants.

Underwater plants are very well adapted to thrive in an environment without much sunlight.

In some ways, living in water is an advantage for a plant. The cells of underwater plants can absorb nutrients and gases, including both water itself and carbon dioxide, directly from the water. There is no need for a layer of cells devoted to reducing transpiration. Underwater plants tend to have leaves that are thin, narrow, and very flexible. They move freely with the movement of the water. They do not grow thick stems or leaves that might obstruct the movement of water, because moving water brings them a fresh supply of nutrients and carbon dioxide gas. Because underwater plants do not need to absorb water and nutrients through their roots, the roots that they have can be shallow. Roots need only anchor the plant in a particular spot.

Since the amount of sunlight available to water plants is greater the closer they get to the surface, these plants tend to adapt in ways that allow them to stay closer to

Without plants to perform photosynthesis, life on Earth would cease to exist.

the surface. Some plants, such as water lilies, grow leaves that float on the water so they can take advantage of full sunlight. Others, such as algae, have no roots at all and live their entire lives floating at the surface. These plants, too, can collect sunlight at its brightest. Many water plants have leaves that can store oxygen. Since oxygen is lighter than water, oxygen trapped in leaves helps them to float or to stay near the surface of the water rather than sinking to the bottom.

Because photosynthesis is critical to the continued survival of life on Earth, scientists study it very carefully. If they could duplicate this process, they could make foods such as beans, grains, and sugars in the laboratory, without having to wait for plants to produce them. They could learn to clean up polluted air by chemically transforming its gases into new substances. Perhaps they could learn new ways to collect, store, and use solar energy. Research of this sort could someday feed the hungry, preserve the environment, and even provide power for the planet.

Glossary

carbohydrate: Food that provides energy to living things.

cells: The small units that make up living things.

chemical process: A process that changes a substance or substances into completely different substances.

chlorophyll: A pigment that collects energy from sunlight.

chloroplast: The organelle where photosynthesis occurs.

guard cells: Cells that regulate the stomata, making sure they are open when they should be and closed when they should be.

photosynthesis: The process by which plants change water and carbon dioxide into food.

rhizomes: Underground stems.

stomata: Small openings in leaves that allow plants to collect carbon dioxide from the air.

succulent: Plant that can collect and store carbon dioxide at night for use during photosynthesis that will occur during the day.

taiga: Land that lies just south of the North Pole tundra.

transpiration: The evaporation of water from the surface of a plant's leaves.

taiga: Land that lies just south of the North Pole tundra.

tundra: Land that remains permanently frozen under a layer of soil.

For Further Exploration

Books

Wendy Baker and Andrew Haslam, *Plants*. Chanhassen, MN: Two-Can, 2000. Part of the Make It Work Science series. Includes activities and experiments.

David Burnie, *Eyewitness: Tree.* London: Dorling Kindersley, 2000. Covers the diversity of locations in which trees grow and how they adapt in different ways to different environments.

Mary M. Cerullo and Bill Curtsinger, *Sea Soup: Phytoplankton.* Gardiner, ME: Tilbury House, 1999. This book focuses on tiny floating ocean plants and their importance to Earth.

Laura Howell, Kirsteen Rogers, and Corinne Henderson, *World of Plants.* London: Usborne, 2002. A basic reference book on plants with links to Internet sites.

Web Sites

BiologyMad (www.biologymad.com). "Module 5: Photosynthesis and Respiration" provides detail on the chemical reaction that takes place in photosynthesis for students who want to know exactly what happens and why.

Blue Planet Biomes (www.blueplanetbiomes.org). Includes sections on major Earth ecosystems, with a discussion of how plants and animals adapt to living in each environment.

FT Exploring (www.ftexploring.com/photosyn/chloroplast.html). Includes detailed diagrams of the parts of a leaf and sections on each part of a leaf's cells.

Missouri Botanical Garden (http://mbgnet.mobot.org). Includes sections on biomes, including tundra, taiga, desert, and grassland ecosystems.

Science Made Simple (http://photoscience.la.asu.edu/photosyn/education/colorchange.html). Includes a detailed description of how plants prepare for winter, and science experiments to try.

Index

Picture Credits

Cover image: © Corel Corporation
© Corel Corporation, 24 (top and bottom), 32
Robert Halstead/Lonely Planet Images, 37
© Danny Lehman/CORBIS, 14
PhotoDisc, 21, 28
Photos.com, 16 (all), 18, 36
© Rick Price/CORBIS, 35
© David Samuel Robbins/CORBIS, 12
© Mark L. Stephenson/CORBIS, 17
© Tom Stewart/CORBIS, 7
© Stone by Getty Images, 38
Keren Su/Lonely Planet Images, 23
© Brant Ward/San Francisco Chronicle/
    CORBIS, 29
Steve Zmina, 11, 26

About the Author

Bonnie Juettner is a writer and editor of children's reference books and educational videos. Originally from McGrath, Alaska, she currently lives in Kenosha, Wisconsin. This is her eighth book.